How Shadows Are Bundled

Mary Burritt Christiansen Poetry Series

MARY BURRITT CHRISTIANSEN POETRY SERIES
V. B. PRICE, SERIES EDITOR

Also available in the University of New Mexico Press Mary Burritt Christiansen Poetry Series:

Poets of the Non-Existent City: Los Angeles in the McCarthy Era
edited by Estelle Gershgoren Novak

Selected Poems of Gabriela Mistral edited by Ursula K. Le Guin

Deeply Dug In by R. L. Barth

Amulet Songs: Poems Selected and New by Lucile Adler

In Company: An Anthology of New Mexico Poets After 1960
edited by Lee Bartlett, V. B. Price, and Dianne Edenfield Edwards

Tiempos Lejanos: Poetic Images from the Past
by Nasario García

Refuge of Whirling Light by Mary Beath

The River Is Wide/El río es ancho: Twenty Mexican Poets, a Bilingual Anthology
edited and translated by Marlon L. Fick

A Scar Upon Our Voice by Robin Coffee

CrashBoomLove: A Novel in Verse by Juan Felipe Herrera

In a Dybbuk's Raincoat: Collected Poems by Bert Meyers

Rebirth of Wonder: Poems of the Common Life
by David M. Johnson

Broken and Reset: Selected Poems, 1966 to 2006 by V. B. Price

The Curvature of the Earth
by Gene Frumkin and Alvaro Cardona-Hine

Derivative of the Moving Image by Jennifer Bartlett

Map of the Lost by Miriam Sagan

¿de Veras?: Young Voices from the National Hispanic Cultural Center
edited by Mikaela Jae Renz and Shelle VanEtten-Luaces

A Bigger Boat: The Unlikely Success of the Albuquerque Poetry Slam Scene
edited by Susan McAllister, Don McIver, Mikaela Renz, and Daniel Solis

A Poetry of Rememberance: New and Rejected Works
by Levi Romero

The Welcome Table by Jay Udall

How Shadows Are Bundled

Anne Valley-Fox

Dear Lisa —
In honor of our luminous Chris,
and your healing love.
Thank you, + love,
Anne Valley-Fox

University of New Mexico Press

November, 2009

Albuquerque

Printed in the United States of America

14 13 12 11 10 09 1 2 3 4 5 6

Library of Congress Cataloging-in-Publication Data

Fox, Anne Valley.
How shadows are bundled / Anne Valley-Fox.
p. cm. — (Mary Burritt Christiansen poetry series)
ISBN 978-0-8263-4781-7 (cloth : alk. paper)
1. Shadow (Psychoanalysis)—Poetry.
I. Title.
PS3556.O876H68 2009
811'.54—dc22
2009020094

Designed and typeset by Mina Yamashita.
Composed in Minion Pro, an Adobe Original typeface
designed by Robert Slimbach, and display type in
Origami Std designed by Carl Crossgrove

For Tom

We meet ourselves in a thousand disguises

along the path.

—Carl Gustav Jung

Contents

IV. Chicxulub

Foreword

Poets can sometimes become hands in the dark for their readers during times of crisis, loneliness, or confusion. If you are looking for a poet to befriend you with her work, Anne Valley-Fox, in *How Shadows Are Bundled*, can become that rare friend on the page who is at once a wise guide and a bracing companion who always takes your side.

In a poem like "The Sadness of Longing," she explores "Something seared in the tender loam of the psyche / so overgrown with trampled grasses / that even a private detective (the crumpled adult / you've become) misdiagnoses / the problem. . . ." But Anne Valley-Fox can be trusted not to see life wrongly.

Many of the poems in *How Shadows Are Bundled* explore what C. G. Jung called "the Shadow," that dark, usually hidden part of each of us, and perhaps the troubled vortex of most group identities when they swerve out of control. W. H. Auden, a poet of conscience aware of the shadow, once said that he reads a poem in two ways, first as a verbal object to be understood and second as an expression of the kind of person a poet is.

In these poems, the verbal objects have a thrilling clarity to them, carrying the reader along into familiar but unexplored and expansive realms that make sense to our deepest feelings. There are few generalities here; the poems are alive with detail. They range from poems about politics, cancer, and spiritual struggles to hurricanes, asteroids, aging, and the work of other writers and film makers. A poem called "Love in the Afternoon" ends: "Like a dream or a scene in a movie / Behind me a queue of refugees. . . . / Miraculously I can see every face / Each keen emotional note approaching crescendo / Death laughs (although not unkindly) as I weep."

The poems reveal the person who created them to be someone with a hard eye and a deep kindness, someone who refuses to turn away from trouble and pain, an unflinching witness who sees the truth but never runs from delight when she finds it. "No love can be discounted," she writes in the book's last poem "Chicxulub," named for the giant asteroid that "tore through the earth's atmosphere / gouging the sea . . . / searing on impact Cretaceous fishes . . . / Tyrannosaurus gnashing samurai teeth. . . ." In a poem about the film *Pan's Labyrinth*, she writes, "Sometimes you have to put your faith in whatever / shows up, something visibly absent / or too grotesque to detect at moments other / than this one in which you are lost, / abandoned by father and mother / cast down lucid with terror. . . ." Anne Valley-Fox is a poet you can put your faith in never to abandon the shadows before they are witnessed and their full story is told.

—V. B. Price
Albuquerque, New Mexico

I

Psyche

Three Martinis

Each night the bartender spirits the napkins home
and stacks them on top of the others like a book.
Tonight the square beneath the novelist's first martini
is marked with a bar graph crowned with rays, as
a lighthouse or phallus. The second napkin, rolled at
one edge, bears the words: *Wm. James—feeling as*
a legitimate form of the rational. After an hour, a third
napkin floats the martini glass—pitched roof in delicate
strokes, grasses penciled high around a barn. And
scribbled slantwise across it: *Is meaning inserted*
or found there?

Summer evenings the writer breaks from the bar to
slurred melon pastels. Tonight a snowstorm has soundlessly
changed the world. A pickup truck leaving the lot turns
too wide and mounts the sidewalk, missing the lone
pedestrian by a breath. The walker walks on, carrying
snow on his shoulders. A coward summons failure before
the finish . . . and what of his protagonist? Character
determines fate, yet in the realm of behavior, substitutes
are sometimes accepted—a tigress held in captivity nurses
a piglet . . . the third martini delivers you over the falls
in a barrel . . . a breakthrough may still be possible.

Pan's Labyrinth
(After the film by Guillermo del Toro)

Sometimes you have to put your faith in whatever
shows up, something visibly absent
or too grotesque to detect at moments other
than this one in which you are lost,
abandoned by father and mother
cast down lucid with terror
woods mined with explosives
slugs big as your fists
bloodshot eyes slit in a vampire's palms.
Hampered by what is entrusted
innocent yet of consequence
like Eve or Persephone plucking forbidden fruits
volatile bundles of Yes and No, briefly
you treasure knowledge.
Because you have chosen the long arc of impossible good
the bird of prana flies from your chest
and red shoes light the stones of the labyrinth.

Man in Box

Major exits along the border manned with AK-47s
Insiders know the system is bankrupt
Stripped of ammo it's down to Russian roulette
But any advantage cancels itself
He charges himself: you lack the will to cross

A girl on the Teen Page is quoted as saying
"I'd rather be hit by a Mack truck than be fat"
His teeth rattle like dice in a cup
The doctor prescribes an antidepressant
He keeps the lid on refusing to leave the house

Shattered jar of sweet syrup his girlfriend's voice
Pricks his skin where it touches
He pushes it back from his body
Muzzy and disembodied
"Honey I'm sorry" or is it "Money I'm starving"?

For twenty-four hours the phone doesn't ring
Swaddled in cobweb it's just as well
No one insists he exists
Saturday night telemarketers call
He picks up the phone and the line goes mechanically dead

Exhausted by sleep on Sunday morning
He plods to the market
Lungs and heart pumping okay at last
The sun asserts itself—oh the lovely arches and toes
Of spring girls in flip-flops!

Ably he chooses: lamb chops, chocolate, wand of chard
But walking home *chi* drains from his limbs

The lock resists the key
He leaves the bag on the kitchen counter
And crawls into bed

Time Magazine's cover this week
A checkerboard of fresh faces—thirty-two dead including
The shooter—like any given day in Iraq—
His solar plexus lifts slightly by clumsy comparison
Light drains from the room as blood from the body

Monday morning he buttons up for the office
Homo sapiens/Talking heads
He commandeers his computer
Eyes florescent by afternoon
Seized by exhaustion he suddenly wants to weep

White boxes flapped open like beached dinghies
His girlfriend clicks enamel chopsticks
He battles for semblance
Words stumble heavy as corpses
His job is simply to speak—

"The stock market rallied without me" he tries to erase
The complaint—"Someone has strung combat boots
And ballet slippers over the power lines—"
His smile is crooked he thinks of fireflies trapped in a box
Yellow light eked from their dying bodies

Imagine a Woman

Of Russian and French descent
much of her life lived on the outskirts of Paris
the child reads with a butterfly net
the schoolgirl exchanges Catholicism for sex
her college studies severed by war
she joins the French Resistance
marries a freedom fighter
after the baby is born he dashes off to foreign wars
she tucks her head, regains some ground
marries again, an older man who calls her Paloma
a master of touch he fixes clocks and watches
a baby comes and quickly another
she teaches piano lessons
the boys grow faster than they can eat
slamming the door, the girl leaves home in search
of her father—Oh, the shock—
her husband's form fallen to the floor!
The widow studies attention
contentment takes her by surprise
the boys leave home and hardly look back
until their babies are born
smooth packets of joy
her last lover she keeps a secret
she prays for her children
give them doors in their hearts with oiled hinges
her children are shocked to see her face
its rivers and canyons
from time to time she studies herself in a mirror
like monks at prayer in the charnel house
the lizard skin bag of her body
but inside the casing she's just sixteen
the young assume her mind is shot
one last autumn she ponders the glassy maple
each leaf seeking the ground
imagine the air on the back of her neck
except for the chill like the satin breath of a lover

The Island

So we live, and are forever leaving.
—Rainer Maria Rilke

The sea is warm and undisturbed. The dreamer could swim
the distance to the island; instead she grabs hold of a rope
dropped from a copter's steel belly and dangles across the water.

A stone building with glass eyes crowns the tiny island.
The dreamer crosses the threshold and enters a ballroom, its air
of profound desertion. A woman in an antique gown,
black for mourning, trails behind the dreamer.

A hallway of padlocked doors wings into a dining hall
where inmates stand, alone or in changeable sets.
Food steams in aluminum trays, but nobody eats.

A play is in play at the far end of the room; a handsome man
with a sonorous voice delivers a soliloquy. The play
dissolves and the smiling actor approaches the dreamer.
He's no more crazy than I am, she muses.

Others collect and move away, drifting in slow motion.
Only their insularity, detached abstraction familiar to the dreamer,
gives them away. Who among them belongs to the world
and who will never connect?

In the end it's an elderly man, blinking into the hard light,
who waves a vague farewell and turns his back on the island.
The silent dreamer watches from her window.

Hypothesis

The way you are cradled in sleep

Like a babe in the womb

Corpse swaddled in rose petals

Seething bed of crustaceans

Embrace of a boy in the back seat of a Ford

Sea of sunned meadow grasses

Cockpit cocoon above the Rio Grande

Sandstone dish of the White Place

Mozart's starry recording booth

The coastline of your beloved's back

Your planet's galactic skin:

It may be the universe loves you

Unlike Alice (Whose Tumble Is Wondrous)

Unlike Alice (who chatters, telescopes, bobs in her tears,
emerging in time for tea)—the real girl who falls in a hole,
gouged and slicked by a hunter,
breaks when she hits bottom.

If she cries out, who will come?

Awake when she sleeps and vice versa,
her body with its clandestine agenda slides into
the dark shape of a woman.

The village women notice her absence and lower a rope.
We are your helpers. These are the steps.
Here is a new set of clothes.

She breaks from their circle and sleepwalks back, hovering
at the brink. The village healer gleans her secrets
and holds them—

all except the one that can't be spoken.

Psyche at Eighteen

(i)
Her dark skin swallows available light
spinning a smooth cocoon around her
a man of her faith but older
pulls her down a road in a wagon
the sides of the wagon dent her hips
he is talking about the life he will give her
she pictures a set of nesting eggs
painted shells fitted into each other
and inside the smallest
a cloth doll folded in darkness
she sings to the radio all day long
waiting for him to come with food and water

(ii)
His voice the color of bruises worms into her ear
I love you I'm going to make you my wife
she clutches the phone
the brass ring on the merry-go-round
mechanically lifting and dropping
he talks and talks
the dry hot gusts of his breath
I want to go to college she says
I'm not ready to marry but he is inhaling
the wasted fragrance around her body
she's tried to pick the prettiest horse its one lifted knee
the carousel ceiling whirling violets and roses

(iii)

After he leaves for work she goes to the closet
and sits in a pile of shoes
hugging her knees to her chest
why does she do this she only knows
ease of cessation
no one will see she is ruined
the leaky seal where sex comes in is tamped down
after sex her husband whispers
nobody else will ever love you the way that I do
his fingers pressing purple stains on her arms
nobody else will ever love you
no one will ever love you

The Sadness of Longing

Something seared in the tender loam of the psyche
so overgrown with trampled grasses
that even a private detective (the crumpled adult
you've become) misdiagnoses
the problem, searching for clues in pop
psychology, pouncing on easy solutions—
take for instance the drunken father
who opens the girl like a package, clumsily
rummages, slaps her together again—
you can jump on the bandwagon, slogans
blared from loudspeakers
bystanders waving miniature flags
but this is not your parade
you've broken the code in the wrong language
your father's love was a loneliness, child—
think of a snow angel pressed into snow, frozen
outline of absence.

Sufficient in Her Skin

She stands beside the car, her arms and chest bare as swans
smooth under the sun's interrogation.
In sixty years she never enlisted the sun as her lover;
she didn't long to change color
or fade to another body.
Cool abstractions the likes of Greta Garbo did not confuse her.
She studied the luminous skin of the world,
the choked green of cedars,
the slow collapse of a haystack.
She painted water and teacups falling over Tiananmen Square.
The family dog died twice in her arms.
Turned inward she notes the folded accordion of karma,
the triple tones of *Ohm*.
When trouble comes she meets it discreetly: "I hope to avoid
the wild emotions of others."

Ashes

Forfeiting the plane ticket I circled back to the warehouse
unless he'd collapsed he'd be easy to spot
I hunted for him
up and down aisles of second-hand goods
racks of clothing
fleets of pots and pans
greeting cards in a basket
stuffed animals missing a limb or an eye
cemeteries of cheap vases and jam glasses
if I continue your eyes will glaze over
not so the shuttle driver
he keeps a clipboard of forms on the passenger seat of his van
and in between runs to the airport
he lists every object on every shelf
in each drawer of the house
string
cotton balls
horseradish
spoons
nothing's too small for the record
it hurts like hell to remember he said
he and his family up to their shins in cinders
he'd hoped to find the dog's tag or even a link of his chain
but nothing survived at 2,000 degrees
this story was going to tell of a man collapsed in a warehouse
instead it's a story of ashes

Catch and Release

Once out of the closet (an actual cranny, stale suits
and dangling necktie nooses)
it wasn't the custard embrace of women she wanted
no it was men in their beautiful bodies
their minds like mineral quarries
wistful and reckless and crude
she knew how to cross a room and make them want her
the rolling stone
the family man pinned by Lilliputians
the spiritual master witching fissures
it wasn't salvation but clout she was after
like generals plotting foreign wars
she'd bully the natives into submission and leave them
once a stranger scooped her out of a green hole
she lay in his hands swollen and gold as a carp
that time she trembled before she leapt
if downstream another fisher could catch her
it was because she would let him
sometimes she played at catch and release
twice hooked she'd flip back into the river
drifting down the dark caves of the current
beached one day in the brown waters of Matamoros
she knelt and kissed the ground
her children like pea plants climbing into the blue
she lay down and the earth curved to hold her

Because You Are Female

Because you are female and psyche is born from the body
you can't imagine how it would feel (and feeling cracks
the seedpod containing the word)
to live in a male body
especially the years when a boy is rocketing into a man
you can't even name the arid or tropical causes of his arousal
under cover of darkness or cloth
athletic organ engorges at random
while female excitement sparks in the mind
a rosy idea flushing neural pathways
spiraling down to the sanctum
thighs warm as bread from an oven
tongue soft in its cave
intuitive art the transposition of inner and outer
she readies herself to translate the force of his nature
and if her agenda is pleasure or procreation
it's all right how afterwards (even if later remorseful)
they split apart like cells in the bloodstream
streaming

Her Suitors Come Crashing

Penelope spins night into day
avoiding the gaze

of would-be rescuers,
wards of the sea

crashing her threshold
their eyes

scalded with shipwreck
and fallen stars.

Different the stranger
down from the hills—

his arms cradling
nightshades and roots

his lotus eyes
quiet on the pond.

Wife of Odysseus
opens the scullery door.

Come in, she says,
show me what you bear.

Smoke Gets in Your Eyes

The girls padded their bras with taffeta strips
torn from slips in the attic and wore them to the dance
polished linoleum winked up their twirling skirts
the boys stared at girl-thighs smooth as new highways
the boys with sunburned noses and hands like mitts
the spinning bottle a green needle coming to rest
behind the curtain split-second decisions
much as later when girls got the pill though you never
know what people are doing behind closed doors
how blithely she drops her clothes her mother's ideas
does he disclose his game is there laughter or lack
Johnny Mathis intended the thing his voice was doing
girl and boy smoky-eyed cheek to cheek do you have
pencils in your pocket she said

Bad Dream

Oh I was alienated to borrow a term
from the era when Sartre and de Beauvoir
lived across the street from each other
the group like a threshing machine and I
refusing to eat the food at their table
not that I was existentially free
you understand or sure of my actions
I suffered from self-inflicted wounds (where
does an action originate?) just let me lick
my wounds my wounded self was saying
the shade of a hangman's tree
even a motionless river would comfort me now
their mouths around the long table
bands of unanimous condemnation did they
see me slip from the room like a thief?

Peace Plan

"There is a simple way to put an end to the random killings ravaging this community," the speaker tells us. A hushed crowd of cutthroats and victims listens intently. "Everyone has a driving fear. Each of you must identify yours; then search for someone who isn't bewitched by that emotion and join forces." Like square dancers lining up in the barn, we locate our partners just as the fiddles are striking up "Chicken in the Straw." The sheriff's homicidal brother, the last person to come around, purrs like a kitten beside his new sidekick. The community van has a fresh coat of paint. We ride out to a sunny meadow and loll on blankets spread with picnic provisions. If this were a movie, they'd pull back the camera and roll the credits. But I am alarmed by ominous shadows gathered along the tree line. I look to my partner, whose laughing mouth is stained red with wine.

Remorse on Occasion

Remorse on occasion
pierces phenomena—
bloody piles of tangled flesh,
ligament messed
beside the road, one feast
for hyenas remarkably
like another—

All dressed up with no place
to go, most of the time
you scratch
a circumference,
furnish a niche, aim to be
steady and true—

But stripped as if suddenly
down to the bone . . . don't
you wish you'd been
more of a piece—bolder, shrewder—
more like the loon, howling
at the watery moon
for the hell of it?

Please Can You Spare Me a Kiss, Walt Whitman?

(i)
Illicit lover says in a dream, *Now you are mine*
instead of his and I say, *No, now I have two lovers*
we walk on a cliff where a bonfire blazes
earlier he was stroking my thigh under a café table
of course I faked a sort of resistance
the way a blade of grass is required
to bruise itself breaking ground
the earth is pleased but she pouts a little for show—
Was that so hard? she teases

(ii)
After his lover leaves him, Walt Whitman
counts the incalculable losses—a book, a war, his beloved—
he sobs into the unwashed sheets of his narrow bed
a shepherd whose flock is lost to the wolves
lies face down in the grass
desire in solitude, geysers arcing toward eros
the lover drags his three-legged grief to the war hospital
where hundreds of soldiers lie dying
their young bodies threshed by munitions
only a few with strength enough to weep
he kisses each man on the lips and sits beside him
holding his hand as long as it takes to die back into grass
sighing under the tender soles of his boots

(iii)
There the poet's slant circumference of light
haloed above his beloveds
the face of an angel
cooling their anguish
their bodies like burnt fields—
Please can you spare me a kiss, Walt Whitman?
me and my paramour clasping stolen trophies
already indifferent to each other
straggling along the precipice in such darkness

Restraint

Carp plump with orange atoms
holds mystically still beside the knife on the cutting
board—once the blade slides in,
oblivion.

The Man in the Mirror

I wake in a room on the fourth floor—iron
balcony, April light—and stand in the bathroom
looking into the mirror. My body has blown
apart in the night like a pile of sand. Livid with
loathing, I pack my bag, quit the hotel and
hail a cab for the airport. At home I regretfully
tell my wife, I no longer love you, I'm leaving.
How can it be that the more she weeps, the more
my flesh firms in the morning mirror?

We Dream in the Dark

On the run and no idea where the train is going, every commuter's
closed face is a mirror.
Chartreuse grasses glow in a field of snow.
Hot tar sucking your knees and the killer is gaining.
You find your stolen Florentine ring under a bowl of rice.
A man you despise when you are awake is a genius of love in bed.
Wet leaves refuse to peel from the glass.
The bride's mother drags her, sobbing, from room to room.
Yours is the saddest task on earth: you must stab the children
to spare them the enemy's wrath.
Night after night the flight to Moscow leaves without you.
Waiting to die on the desert floor—how peaceful you feel
beside the blooming primrose!
The secret to joy is gobbledygook when you wake.
A mushroom cloud burgeons behind your firstborn's head: "Pack up
your toys, Sweetheart, we're heading home."
Desperate to cover your nakedness, you struggle to pull on pants
made of rubber, two sizes too small.
Overvoice: "All beings are linked in a circle."
Wake up laughing: Orange juice can with orange background and blue
block letters: "Noodle Soup."
Your old dog, back from the dead, asks you to walk her.
There's nothing strange about breathing underwater.
You come to a campsite where every stranger is deeply in love with
every other—a sweetness you'll never forget.

How Shadows Are Bundled

A last dance a swig from the jug to slur the kiss
"Maybe I'll marry the outlaw I've always loved him"
you say to someone who isn't listening
"Don't be an ass" the psyche shouts loud enough to wake you
the psyche knows how shadows are bundled
curled petals beneath forsythia bushes
leave them alone deciduous mulch December's communion wafers
you'd think the spook in the attic would have dissolved by now
barely a woman you stepped into the virginal tepee of shadow
the slanted walls were suffocating
maybe you died or did you breathe through hairline cracks in the ice
time goes retro and speeds up again
the iceman is sent to prison for blue-collar crime
you get your shadow back it's stunningly heavy
how about cutting it into pieces swallow them one at a time
or run away on an airplane
the stewardess lets you follow her home to Arlington for a night
DC our city of deepest shadow
you fade into others the outline of envy riding the bus after work
"Power to the People!" fisted on buildings in East LA
the suicide-grey surf of Manhattan Beach
the wrong celebrities are assassinated
a lace tablecloth scallops your bay window in San Francisco
light and fog like pearl buttons down the front of a dress
your body a maple someone can tap with a bucket
a baby crying deconstructs the seductive voices of poets
the university of children
you may not graduate
you hang your cloak like a fool on a manikin's shoulders
backstage the conjurer's aspect is haggard
"I want to be alone"

the wrecking ball hauled from the basement glints copper lights
you choose a partner who smiles when you come into the room
cast your vote the same way
waltz on the wedding cake steps of the New York Public Library
up and down and diagonally
he takes the steps at full speed from top to bottom
your limbs twining his torso your hair sheeted high like a sail

II

Things That Want to Be Counted

Up in the Dark

Put your feet on the floor Joko Beck said
it's the hardest part of the Zen thing
to wrest your body away from its dream clutches
sit on your zafu
cowboy asleep on his horse
stone Buddha awake in the dark
thieving morning concentrates attention
bubble by bubble
dawn slips over tenement sills
balloons into rooms
swells the ribs of the radiator
yellow pencil rowing across a sunrise lake
everything flashing molecular presence
light photons illumine the bowl
you get up and speak to the goldfish—hello
my beauties!—change their green water

At the Movies with Singing Shoe and Two Bodhisattvas

Seat backs and wooden ladder leading up to concessions
sticky from so many hands, I've folded into a seat
with a bird's-eye view of the screen, when my left shoe begins
to sing in a leathery bebop contralto.

A young man seated behind me leans forward and speaks
to the shoe. "You're quite the crooner, aren't you, pal?
Listen to you!" He touches his lips to the side of my neck
in a kiss so tender it bends the arc of the universe.

The shoe falls into contented silence. The young man
and his girlfriend beside him are smiling when I swivel around
to see them. "What in this world," I answer them,
"does not respond to kindness?"

The movie is clearing its throat and we all settle in
for *It Happened One Night* with Claudette Colbert, spoiled
darling who needs to be spanked, and Clark Gable,
the perfect man for the job.

Chris's Tresses

When Chris was ten she decided never to cut her hair again.
In high school her tresses, sandy brown with surfer-girl
streaks, fell in waves to her knees.

When Chris comes into a room you notice her hair, flowing
like water along her willowy body.

Chris built a studio in the country and later a house
with pitched tin roof. She straddled the roof, hammer glinting,
hair coiled around her head like a basket of lights.

Every day she braids or wraps, sweeping her hair
out of the way of kilns and vats of clay.

After a bath, in summer or fall, sometimes
Chris sprawls on the ground beside her hair in the sun.

Now she must tell her beloveds: a tumor
the size of a chicken egg bullies a number of vital organs
huddled near the raw place where her uterus was.

She knows that chemo will tug her hair from the roots.
Strand by strand it will fall onto sheets, collect in the tub,
curl into autumnal nests on her sweetheart's shoulders.

Chris laughs with tears in her eyes. "Okay, I'll be bald
as a baby's ass—but with any luck, I'll live."

Chris in June

Chris and I rest on a bench at the foot of the stupa
shaded by grandfather cottonwood trees
and lines of colored cloth.
We've come to soak up the silent rustle
of hundreds of prayer flags
under the golden dome.
Chris pulls off her red scarf and runs a hand
feelingly over the stubble.
This morning she lay in the steel mouth
of an x-ray machine
struggling to calm her breath.
I feel her emotion surge and retreat
like tides in a deep lagoon.
"Now what I pray for," she says, "is a steady heart."

Chris in the Light

The fleshy lump at the mouth of her cave
charred now by cleansing fires
is x-ed off the screen like a kiss.
She hails the old cat—"Skidmark, I'm going to live!"
He blinks his good eye.
The hardware clerk, kindly neighbor
who watched her scalp appear like a moonscape
over the winter months, sells her a digging shovel.
She shovels debris from the ditch.
She picks apples and pears from her orchard,
abundance left for the birds
and bulging bags on her friends' doorsteps.
Her new set of tires comes with a five-year warranty.
The earth around her house she prods
with morning glory and hollyhock seeds—hurrah!
She rereads each well-wisher card and feeds it
to the fire. Her right-hand man, impassioned
spokesman during the crises,
collapses, out of steam.
Her mother weeps with pent up grief and relief.
The oncologist cites his patient's triumph over a rogue
tumor to certain others he guesses can handle
the long arc of hope.

The rest of her life breathes like clay in her hands.
She sorts the past into scrupulous piles
and makes a run to the dump.
Her former rope of silken hair
comes in coarse and curly.
Gratitude trumps ambivalence now
despite the insidious question: And if cancer
returns to the scene in its lumpy, bespattered coat?

Each extravagant day, the wild horses of light!
A flicker alights in tasseled grass
on the morning mesa. Certain objects
shine directly; others glow
or are backlit like haunted houses. And if
she witlessly drifts into shadow? Pinpoints of light
can be mined, where she finds them, like gold.

Swan Lake

After the funeral, the widow's tiny ballerina bones are
gathered into an armchair. She nibbles a shaving of roast
beef on a round of rye, her first meal in days. Beneath
the maestro's oil portrait over the hearth, his sons pour
scotch all around in their father's honor. Talk dissolves
to city politics, water cisterns, a road trip to Missoula
with the dogs. The dead man's father, a concert violist,
insisted the boy drop out of school when he was sixteen
to spare his hands: all day he could practice his fiddle.
He met his wife on an opera train before the war. For sixty
years he'd tell anyone: her dancer's legs were the best
he had ever seen. The widow's cheek collapses under your
kiss. You can feel her drifting backwards into the cold lake.

Swamplands

(For Ezra)

My oldest son phones me from Manhattan.
He's off the Q from Brooklyn, walking west on Canal,
headed up to the Art Students League.
A helicopter sputters over the avenue.
"How are you, honey?" I ask, meaning something larger.
He answers in the generic.
Sirens overwhelm his voice for several seconds.
We are talking, yet still I long to connect.
In Santa Fe, I watched the Virgin of Guadalupe
effigy in a blue dress, crossing town, borne
on the shoulders of pilgrims.
My son says: "Last weekend I went up to Alexandria Bay
to see my grandma. I love the starkness of the place
and its maternal warmth."
A lullaby calm settles over the city.
I think of a reptile, belly down in the bottoms,
so long I have loved him.

Attention

You're not here to learn anything. You're here to let go of things.
—Shunryu Suzuki Roshi

If a single window is all you have to see through
and light pours through it
in heavy woolens
in summer dresses
if other rooms are soundless and dark
as buttressed cathedrals
if all you need to witness is one half of an apple tree—
blossoms in love with the earth
limbs in love with the air—
if once in a blue moon a plane slices a corner of sky
a sparrow's body stunned against the glass
toe-shoed snowflakes thumping black branches
explosion of leaves unfolding
the ceremony of green
the deprivation of green
if you can sit your galloping pony
and not get thrown by other galloping ponies
under the apple tree: a Bodhisattva

Old Cat

His triangular head the soft chassis of his jaw
sinks to your palm
ribs narrowing toward the hips
a long shot of train tracks
skinny child balancing on the rail
too decrepit to reach around and lick his rump
fur spiking like mustard weeds beside the tracks
he seems to perceive density
the liquidity of sunlight
sometimes a drum corps marching in heavy coats
he doesn't purr anymore but stroke his throat
trace the bony ridge of his spine
and he flips into bliss
gravity tugging evenly on all his parts
he doesn't care if dust clots his coat
no regard for pageants of strength or beauty
not even the orange calico slinking across the yard
his dry sneezes are neither good nor bad
he cares about fish (if it's fresh)
his mattress of periwinkles
the weight of your hand is his Beethoven's Ninth
leavened atoms plumping the air
a sweet reprieve from the pale rasp of his voice

Sonnet for My Mailman

October light tinsels the kitchen window. Across
the street my mailman parks, lights a cigarette,
talks on his cell as he smokes. The neighbor's elm
looses leaves onto the roof of his white van. This
carrier's never been friendly to me; of course
there's my dog, her cheap imitation of Cerberus;
plus, I imagine some helpless obsession commands
his ardent protection. I almost said, My mailman
dislikes me—accent on me, shining star of the
universe! He flicks a second butt to the street, his
forearm tanned and shapely as his calves in summer
shorts. He exits the van and shoulders his sack.
Whatever the straits or fictions of mind, my mailman
reciprocates, six days a week, my love.

Sunday Brunch

Santa Fe City Dump announces itself: *Solid Waste Transfer Station*
when Tom and I drive out to look at
Stonefridge:Fridgehenge—
huge, cubed food coffins
Frigidaires, Coronados, Americanas
coiled backs and blank fronts
stacked in a circle like stolid peasants
dancing in a field.

The assemblage strikes me as haughty—
proud of their Schwarzenegger proportions
despite the fact that their license
to chill has expired.
And if they could talk?

Flat, nasal, Jersey inflections:
"Then we were kingpins, major fixtures—
but how about you, chumps?
Haven't you missed the frigate?
All you've got is a shelf life of Sunday mornings!"

* * *

Last week we descended a ladder, stepped beneath the former
civic center into a world
unearthed by archaeologists—
meticulously, with picks and calligraphy brushes
they opened a pithouse dating to the 1300s—
red ochre wall paintings, twin-holed stone altar
shaped as labia, mounds of ashes and masonry vaults
used for storage, maybe also burial.

The city is putting pressure on the State Office of Archaeological Studies
to finish digging, cap their graphs and photographs
            and get out—bulldozers purr in the city lot, poised
    to level Tesuque Pueblo's ancestral sites
for underground parking spaces.

            But science, like love, cannot be rushed.
        The team curves to its labors. "Look how carefully,"
    someone admires, "the people who lived here
filled the postholes before they moved on."

* * *

We wait for a table at Tecolote Café and scan the Sunday
paper—Neighbors and Real Estate sections plump;
five scrawny pages for The Nation and The World.

    Once at an animal park outside of Phoenix
        I watched the feeders hurl hunks of raw meat
            over the tops of the carnivores' enclosures—one
        lioness lay down, her flushed heart drumming the prize
    for several minutes before she devoured the whole of it.

Our waitress delivers hot platters with practiced kindness.
Two eggs pool against posole. Tom ladles maple syrup
over his cakes; his wild brows go up
as he cuts into the stack.

Love in the Afternoon

Love is a dangerous necessity.
—Charles Mingus from *Charles Mingus in Paris*

My sweetheart and I are rolling around one afternoon
Swept along by Beethoven's violin concerto
Yehudi Menuhin peeling back
The red petals of the Allegro ma non troppo
When Death comes into the room
Robed in the key of D major
Imperial cape of thunderbolts and stars
Single pointed he doesn't stand on ceremony
His sonorous voice surges up a staircase and down
"Now you must pay attention"
Our nakedness stretches away like a landscape
The first violin is lifting me up on gold threaded arpeggios
My playmate's fingers trail my spine as I leave the bed
Larghetto in G streaming along a cobblestone street
Dark-stained by eighteenth-century burghers
Blood and smoke glossed with cakes of soap
Double stops chain my ribs in a fierce embrace
Coaxing containment of beauty and grief
A locomotive waits in the station swathed in blue smoke
Like a dream or a scene in a movie
Behind me a queue of refugees
Skylight rays glossing the tops of their heads
Some tote a basket or box
The rondo stretches out the door and around the block
Miraculously I can see every face
Each keen emotional note approaching crescendo
Death laughs (although not unkindly) as I weep

Writing a Poem

The jazz musicians take a break from broken time in Lydian groove
I should have refused when someone asked me to read some poems
despite the jazzy oxygen   I'm wrung dry   the podium is oppressively
narrow   I flip through a clutch of manuscript pages I've never seen
before   like crazy people come to the door demanding you say their
names   whining you promised to love them   it's my sick addiction
to freshness   if only I remembered the words   the audience is sleepy
their lids at half-mast   what the hell   I settle on something to read
a short list of historical dates typed in stingy letters   and under this
Tyrants and Lovers which might have segued to helmets or poisonous
flowers but nothing follows and so I continue turning pages   an old
friend's jealous lover dumped a five-pound bag of flour over his typer
he picked up a pen and didn't stop writing except to throw her out
I might have cited TV snow or pear blossoms   a poem decides for itself
the tidy stalls of punctuation (a well-placed period Coleridge wrote
like a spike to the heart)   you have to know what you're imitating   test
the springboard   one word selected over the others   Miss Switzerland
no wait I've changed my mind   Miss Venezuela makes more of a splash
we're talking the Universe here   gestures intended but not results
the audience stays in their seats   lazy more than expectant   they've
given up on me   the Poetry Guard should take me out and shoot me
I go on perversely flipping pages and ten people are killed in a market
in Baghdad   all of them innocent of everything

Remembering Creeley

This a multiple poetry; no one owns it.
—Robert Creeley

Tigress sun slinks under
the vineyard's
awning—
New Mexico poets (&
one Texan)
mount the platform—
language licks
jazz riffs
stories & poems &
weather's wild sweetness
not to mention
Creeley's own extravagant
nature (the bounce
the visceral beat of his
breath)—we're all at once
on a first-name
basis with
Bob.

*

Napes of our necks
sun-licked, cocked
to listen
flies mate midair
poets pitch Creeley riffs
into autumn's savage
smile, the lovely
dying light.

*

Winter of '73 (or '4?
still the rabid dog of war
in Vietnam)

Creeley's
fans
waited for him
half an hour at St. Mark's
in the Bowery
at last his charged
arrival
(also a patch over the gone
eye) promising
danger—rat-a-tat-tat!
he fired off a few lines
& stopped
abruptly—
easy enough
for us to forgive (stoned
on something or
other), our genius his excess—
too drunk
to read his own
words.

*

Somewhere Creeley sd
he stumbled into
a poem,

by which I imagine
any
poem
a kinetic
slate, template to re-
arrange yr head, glue
the confetti
another
way together.

*

Down he went
rowing
his boat
divested of baggage (packed
grief at our pinched,
as he called it,
world)
proverbial bubble in a stream—
remember he sd
there's no use in counting.

*

Full moon slides along
I-25
rabbit or man
regards us coolly as if
attempts
to distinguish ourselves
to shore up
kindness
or beauty against
brutality—
all fall equally by
the wayside.

—Placitas, New Mexico, September 2005

Reading Mary Oliver

He makes a papery racket
searching for the perfect bag
to carry Japanese cups to his daughter
on an airplane tomorrow.

Disturbance of lilacs, corner dust, his quiet
bachelor rooms—the black snake
on a summer road, its
crushed cells gleaming.

A Place in the Desert
(For MQB)

(i)
Quetz is telling about her trip to the desert.
We're giving a new café downtown
a run for its money,
coconut milk sipped from the nut,
Gado-gado, Singapore noodles, dead of winter
in Santa Fe, sunshine in the Mojave.

She's telling about a guy she met in Yucca Valley
car mechanic, a friend of friends,
Volkswagen skeletons parked in his yard;
Special Forces in Vietnam
had trained him to ambush the mind
as well as the body.

Quetz said he'd take an object fixed in a room
and move it slightly when you were away
to make you think
you were crazy.

He suffered a slew of ills, poor guy, a hole in the gut
and he couldn't get it up anymore
(though he touted his
lesbian virtues).

His name was Frank but Quetz called him Francisco.
She cut him some slack, paid his back Gas and Electric
and spent a series of nights in his dive
smoking weed and listening to tirades on situations
blanched in the dry mouths of ghosts.

So after a couple of weeks
when Quetz told Frank she was going home
and wouldn't be taking him with her
he slumped in his armchair of torn guitars
and cried.

(ii)
Meanwhile Quetz and her oldest friends
drove down the Morongo Valley
upthrust and spiked with yucca
to Desert Hot Springs.

Entrepreneurs had pushed out the Indians,
opened a spa for the Hollywood crowd
in the '30s or '40s—

the sacred grounds were nearly deserted:
steaming ponds flanked by boulders,
blossom-studded water lilies, black
swans and gold-flashing
koi—

Here Quetz slows the narration . . .
mango sherbet icing our tongues, we're stunned to remember
our forfeited souls—

how bold and luminous they once were,
vials for pouring light.

The Summer Pages
(For Kalu)

Stained with soil and ink, pages of love and confusion.
Her son's bed tousled from sleeping, from not sleeping.

Her car is frowzier now, one hubcap clattered over an edge;
of course I'll replace it, he says.

He drives one-handed, look Ma, the other working his iPod.
Don't smoke in the car, she says, it sullies my ecosystem.

The first two weeks she snuffs out spontaneous
fires, her leaping flames of impatience.

How is your job search coming? strikes him as an ambush.
Hit Parade parenting rule #5: Choose your battles.

Last summer's girlfriend slips into his room after midnight.
Her silvery laugh like Lady Chatterley running in the rain.

Later the front door brushes the swollen threshold.

Out of the blue a job comes up, clearing brush on a ranch.
He borrows a pair of work gloves from his stepfather.

Dig holes. Clean stalls. Eradicate cholla on 2,000 acres.
A cactus dagger changes his walk, his name to Achilles

Rocks are tossed from man to man down the side of a mountain
to line the millionaire's garden.

Off-loading rocks in the rain, a sore throat ruins his weekend.

At least when you're back at college, his mother laughs,
you'll know what you don't have to do.

Sun torpedoes the ranch, takes no prisoners.
He sweats off the sunscreen by 10 a.m., his forehead a torch.

So what, his skin is only twenty summers old.

She tries to mind her own summery business.
Another mother in quicksand: he is her business, too.

Arguments flare in the name of time, its use and abuse.
At age five he used to say, "You're not the boss of me."

He picks up the six-pound cat and kisses his furred skull,
like sprinkling holy water. What a sweet old cat you are!

Mid-July he's MIA for twenty-four hours.

In the empty morning, she stomps out to the cottonwood sapling
and plugs the earth with sticks of Juicy Fruit gum.

Choke to death, you damn rodents!

Returned home her son is amused, affectionate.

Who is the parent here?
Not the one with the upper hand.

Where did you go? You didn't answer your cell.
He and his friends were out of range

hiking a trail at the ski basin. Coming down,
some homeless campers invited them for supper.

Three old guys in their sixties, hooked up in Colorado,
John and Science and Ghost.

Ghost a Vietnam vet. All three of them skinny and gnarled,
crazy and smart, talking across each other.

What did you eat? Something mushy out of a can, it was dark.
Where did you sleep? Over at Neal's, it was late.

Because she loves her humans too, the story soothes her. And
oh, the car's side-view mirror got smashed in the parking lot.

Around her neck she wears a tablet of things to do with his name
on it. Aboriginal talisman hanging down to her navel.

At noon he hunches over a breakfast burrito while Lisa and Bart
make fools of adults on his laptop.

Now that he's finally out of bed, she expects him to spring into action.
But no, the prefrontal cortex patiently waits for a galvanizing idea.

Keep your anxiety to yourself, everything's under control,
he rebukes her.

Call her Sisyphus. Loose boulders anticipate an avalanche.

The dusky barbeque hunkers under its smoky meat perfume.
After dinner he sketches a drip irrigation system on a napkin.

Four weeks left of summer, of son.
She numbers the precious, exasperating days.

He loses the borrowed gloves and hangs a line of prayer flags
along the front porch.

By early August the vendors are roasting Hatch green chilies
in turning vats in grocery store parking lots.

August 6 and August 9: Little Boy and Fat Man:
200,000 humans incinerated on a summer day.

The door scrapes the threshold at 5 a.m. when he comes home
to sleep.

Things That Want to Be Counted

Someone on earth is counting—
night stars,
rooms in a honeycomb,
snow geese descending, wild
lilies, grain spilled from a bushel basket,
bubbles rising up from a blue hole.

Those who are hungry get up in the dark.
Their job is to count
sticks of kindling, cups of milk,
empty beds or racks of shoes,
newspapers in the dwindling stack,
how many fish in the bottom of the boat.

III

New Math

Barrel of Night

The way wild salmon power up laddered falls
drop their pearls in gravel
and slide downward
or parrots swivel squawking heads
on top of their bright bodies
other species do not distress themselves
with certain exceptions
for instance a modern dancer
spiraling out of contraction
human beings are doomed to review the conditions
good evil boredom dread freedom commitment
who am I where am I going
each decision a fist of dirt gathering into a landslide
who doesn't lie awake in the steel barrel of night
struggling to get things right
the vet on the radio
recently back from Iraq
terrified in his "other mind" he'll lunge at the baby
cut off her fingers whatever else he will do
his mind a pit mine
scraped bald fogged in paranoia
he comes around wrapped in bars or a straightjacket
more than ever afraid of himself
certain trails are treacherous to go back over
who can foresee quicksand traps in a clear stream
a false step you take at twenty that lasts as many years
the one where a child slips underwater
we cling to the lines the spinning compass teased by sirens
calling our secret names

The Falls

Not visible yet but you can hear them
fisted into themselves around the bend
cliff-clawed turbulence spitting mist
the clay muscles around your mouth
and how the mouth would feel if the teeth
were yanked from your head
and how a girl in white strides in a park
her loose limbs permitting
and old men molded to benches
ogle the girls it's their masculine right
and all they can do
and how sometimes you summon a word
easy as calling a child to supper
(plucked corn, the berries of summer)
you call but he doesn't come

Hunger

Porch with missing planks (rictus of pulled teeth)
the back door torn from its hinges

look!—a broken border of rock
the hollow plaid of a scarecrow's sleeve—

here the refugees sink to their knees
(how easy it is to sink)

digging with raw hands
where something must have bloomed—

onions, potatoes, beets—
at least there are tendrils, trailing roots

lovely as lace spread on a table
brimming bowls, a pitcher of cream—

each throat tightens in prayer:
let my fingers strike a tuber, a cluster to go

around—one digger stares at his palms,
cracked, the color of excrement—

even the child's grubbing fists remind him of
something tender and good to eat.

Near Tucker Ponds in a Time of War

Leaves and pine needles dripping rain

Stars resurgent above us

You read to me in the soggy tent

Hoagy Carmichael's rollicking riffs

On Bix Beiderbecke and Louis Armstrong

Licks molten and moonslick

You turn out the lamp

Across the valley a convoy of trucks

Harrows the pass

Reverberant war and its spoils

I cup your ear with my fingers

Treading a moment, softly

Mad Elephants

It is so worthwhile that you devote your precious human life
to controlling your mad elephant mind.
—Lama Yeshe, *Make Your Mind an Ocean*

Under guard at Camp David, metal-chested Generals,
Purple Hearts and scrubbed

hands, are locked in private council with the President.
Big Brass and *Enfant Terrible*, their own prodigal son.

Out the window, rain strafes the open faces
of eight coral roses.

I've muffled the phone and gagged the Sunday paper.
Half the world will fall to its knees

as we bomb the land of Afghanistan with mad elephants.

History's Path Spirals Down to a Precipice

A woman walking a prison yard is speaking to a CNN reporter.
Yes, she attempted to blow herself up
among a group of Israelis—her husband and brothers

were slain in Jenin and their bodies
could not be retrieved. Yes, her daughters are one and seven—
"But there are many orphaned children in Palestine."

The camera feeds on her bruised beauty and pulls away.
Wistfully, the reporter concludes: "Here is woman in her prime,
attractive, a mother—and yet, her life has been ruined."

Click to change the channel. Here in the land of plenty, the dictates
keep coming: *Buy now, never say die, nothing comes of nothing.*
Only the vanquished, packed into prisons and cemeteries,

lift their gaze as the elders call for the children to jump!
from the walls of their ruined city.

Table Talk

(i)
A family is linked around a table eating by failing light.
The goal is to keep the baby from crying, the fork
from clanging against the porcelain plate.
The grandparents sit like corpses, forsaken; the children
have learned not to speak. Their parents attempt
to silence their heartbeats, as if to prevent Nazi boots,
like waterlogged coffins, knocking against the stairs.

(ii)
Dinner for eight on a patio, a toast to the host!
A neighbor is practicing drum rolls. Someone tells
of a Mexican journey, a win-win bribe, a body shop
in Oaxaca. Another bottle of wine and salmon steaks
from the grill. A straw poll: Hillary vs. Obama (split
down the middle and not by gender). A gust of wind
snuffs out a candle. Talk meanders to indie films,
missing Mollie Ivins, the cat's nine lives.

(iii)
Someone starts out, others fill in the blanks: Guantánamo
Bay, Abu Ghraib (the body knows the exact meaning
of torture), U.S. warships off the coast of Iran,
blood for oil, corporate designs on water and air,
the government's rape of the Constitution (brittle doll,
those are her bones popping)—after a while, no one
present can think of a way to rescue the fallen evening.

(iv)
A 7-Eleven clerk from Chihuahua struggles to understand
"Marlboro Lights." The customer snaps, "I'm from Texas
and we speak English in Texas."
A young man standing behind him breaks in,
"Well, I'm a local and we don't speak Asshole here."
He tells the story at dinner—point or miss?
Something trumps nothing. And still we must learn
to hum in our throats and sting like the honeybee.

Loving Dick Cheney

We also have to work, though, sort of the dark side, if you will.
We've got to spend time in the shadows in the intelligence world.
—Dick Cheney to Tim Russert on *Meet the Press*, September 16, 2001

(i)
Just after the vice-presidential debate, two men from Secret Service
appear at my door. They ferry me to a tract home on the outskirts
of town, lead me to a bedroom behind the kitchen,
and leave me with Mr. Cheney.

(ii)
The VP has divested himself of forty pounds and thirty years.
He's traded his suit and blood red tie for jeans and a work shirt,
sleeves rolled to the elbows. He smiles at me, a person he's never
met, and I notice a space between his front teeth I hadn't seen
on television—or maybe he hadn't smiled. The gap is beguiling
and friendly. We turn down the bedclothes together.

(iii)
We rock in the raft of early morning light. Cheney ignores the
ticktock voices behind the wall. He touches my ear with his lips:
"I lifted off the planet last night and you were my guide. Tell me,
who are you?" I fall to the casual, mocking stance of a younger woman.
"I'm no one you'll ever know . . . my name came up in the lottery.
But you and I make dangerous bedfellows, don't we?"

(iv)
A river of energy surges towards me. "Sweetheart," he urges,
"I need another night with you." I shake my head, no.
"This was arranged for one night only—more, and we start
hurting people." Out the window, honeybee girls cluster in the yard.
"But this is not about anyone else," the VP insists. "It's strictly
personal, something I want for myself."

(v)
"But you don't *have* a self," I explode. "You only have *power*!
Every time you make a move you savage the lives of
innocent people around the—"

(vi)
"Show me," he whispers, extending his beautiful arms.

(vii)
The man blazes with radical tenderness no one has ever touched.
So even as I struggle against him, I'm bargaining
with myself:

If for a night I burn in his hands—
rapture of enemy kiss and caress—
a phoenix may rise from the ashes,
and this: In thirty years—
though love is eclipsed—
he won't attack Iraq.

Things We Can Do

An archaeologist in our town is dying of cancer.
Sighing, Natasha tells her husband
she longs to feel warm, one last time, warm
in the sun near the sea.

You and her other office mates are wondering if
there is time enough to get Natasha
a plane ticket—lift her above the mined turquoise
hills of New Mexico.

I know, fantastically, what I would do.
Tuck her into a station wagon and drive west . . .
she'd wake to morning in the Mojave, hot
sun the colors of hard candy.

Here, the trees are filling with snow.
Asian tsunamis open their mouths and swallow the world.
You blow on my fingers to warm them. There are
tiny, perfect things we can do.

Mazurka

Early morning snow flurry melts
within an hour.

During which, Dream Queen, what did you achieve?

I listened to a crow's mazurka
on a pebble roof.

Notes to a Man Who Is Thinking of Leaving His Wife

You tell me your marriage hangs in the balance, as if you're a man
who lies awake straining to see through the dark.

This is a lie by omission (the verb changes its suit).

Love's fled. You've set the scales and instantly taken measure:
Pan #1 (jammed with thirty years of marriage) floats as if weightless.
Pan #2 (apparently empty) hangs low with racy, imagined shapes.

Already your wife plummets through space in her capsule of dread.
(Let the goddess, who loves her better, stretch out a net.)

Imagination, and nobody else, is your queen.

Nothing before this can keep you—.

Your children have long since packed their bags
and moved to other countries.

Public Opinion (inveterate whore) butters her bread with tits and ass,
then tithes a flashy percentage to the church.

Hermetic Soul locked in his tower is bored by human behavior.
Do as you please—just keep a flame
flickering in the dark.

Your circle of friends is already gapped, a grin with missing teeth.
Some feel betrayed (they thought they knew you).
There's worry about contagion.

I'll bet you saw in a blinding flash that love and death are beloveds.

Not all epiphanies are holy.

Of course it's too late for words . . . and yet I go on.

Freedom is ease in the harness (R. Frost).
Slipped from his fetters, a man may imagine stilettos and satin whips.
Is this what his efforts have earned him?

Every man for himself, then. (We women have moves of our own.)

Your brimming applecart turned on its side doesn't affect
"the whole catastrophe" (Zorba).

My upset is not about you, old friend, but our taste for illusion.
A party magician slips the ace of spades up his sleeve—

how deftly we parlay deceptions and wasted kisses!

At the Hardware Store

She trailed the clerk along an aisle of trowels and adhesives,
noticing how his hips hinged, the trout
epaulettes on his shoulders, holes scorched in his cheeks.

He knew his powers had slipped a little (what middle-aged guy's
had not?) but most of his buddies were dead or in prison
and he could still maneuver the dance floor and coax a rainbow
out of a stream like nobody's business.

Her mind, she realized, had holes like his face (why not, after
so many years?). Instead of learning the uses of things
her attention veered to Imelda's shoes, a seagull dragging a
broken wing, 7,000 languages left to comfort the world.

Contempt

(After Jean-Luc Godard's film, 1963)

There's no room for extras in the streets of this movie
the old Italian village its backdrop of tacked on condos
swells with enormous egos first the doe-like Francesca
translator of languages sauntering toward us down a lane
tracked by movie cameras an opening illusion

of perfect weather her yellow skirt prefigures the yellow robes
the starlets will wear above the turquoise waters of Capri

and Jack Palance the cartoon villain American movie producer
Francesca his lover calls him Jerry a name too genial for him
and Fritz Lang as Fritz Lang director in love with the classics
monocle clenched against his artistic disdain

Michael Piccoli plays Paul the devoted husband
(or so we think until we see the arctic flash of his anger)
and then Bardot stretched slantwise across the marital bed
belly down exquisitely naked a backside worthy of foreplay

Godard the real director makes us wait to see her face
Bardot as Camille toys with her husband in sheeted shadow
"Can you see my feet in the mirror?" "Do they look pretty?"
"Do you like my knees?" "Do you like my ass?"
"Which do you love *le plus*?" and so on in half-lit boudoir French

"*Oui*" he says he loves it all though later he will betray her
the audience is more devoted riding the camera along
Bardot's provocative landscape lovely to anyone even
the callous producer who snatches her up in his sharky teeth
an easy catch she will bleed to death but first

the couple must argue all afternoon they don't know
or do they the gods have already judged them

pacing their rented Italian flat talking through walls
("*Quoi?*" "*Rien!*") the marital noose tightens and slackens

Camille's raven wig her red towel in and out of the tub
she sets the table unsets the table as Paul plays a dressing game
"You don't love me anymore" "Of course I do you say such
stupid things" "You did but you don't" "No and I'll die before

I'll tell you why" Paul steps through an inner door
empty where glass should be
he slaps Camille he says they need to talk
they can't stay in the same room together

he flicks the breasts of a sculpted nude the metal rings
against his fingers our ears are bored with their bickering
going nowhere but still our eyes cling to their bodies
resistant and doomed as our own

Camille's mascaraed eyes black as an enchanted forest
enter at your own risk we would if we could
but only the camera can touch her
close to the wall she denounces Paul pronouncing words
he calls unbecoming the sounds hover in love with her lips

of course they go to Capri the villa's pyramid steps ascend to the roof
Camille crosses the platform in self-conscious barefoot beauty
on all sides the blue Odyssean sea
Paul calls her name agilely zigzagging up the steps

Camille plunges into the sea her porcelain nakedness shot from above
Paul dozes in the sun

of course Camille kisses Jerry the kiss of death *Fin! Voila!*
a trickle of blood is all the emotion Godard permits
he didn't let us love her

Book Report
(After *Them*, a novel by Joyce Carol Oates)

After she wakes to her blonde hair lapping blood
her lover's brains spilled on the pillow beside her

Loretta marries into the Wendall family
at sixteen her mother dead her father a drunk

oh that bastard her brother crazy to kill somebody
better for her to marry the cop than go to prison

Howard's not a bad man she's grateful to him
for getting rid of the mess she gives him sex

and three children Jules Maureen and Betty not that
he wants them especially after he's kicked off

the force for corruption Ma Wendall slinging curses
herds the family out to the country

Loretta's husband signs her father off to the nuthouse
Howard is drafted and disappears from the pages

little Jules runs away every chance he gets
Maureen watches her big brother burn down the barn

Loretta screams at her mother-in-law "Goddamn
old bitch of a horse!" over her shoulder

she and the kids ride a bus overnight to Detroit
Jules and Maureen are scared of the dark buildings
the dark faces of Negroes

no hero's welcome for Howard when he comes back
he hurls a wrench at the goddamn slum plumbing

Loretta baits him sometimes he takes a swing at her
he sits at the table without speaking

why don't they shut the hell up especially his son Jules
(if he's even his son) always something smart to say

Jules especially hates his father's silence
he dreams about freedom and money

and killing his father
(Don't! the reader pleads)

at twelve he's stricken with love for Sister Jerome
she weeps in front of the class

he wants to kiss her fingers on the piano keys
no one objects when Jules drops out of high school

underage he stocks shelves at the five-and-dime
his father is crushed at the plant by two tons of steel

Maureen goes numb watching her father die
her mother's sloppy emotion the hospital's stink of death

Loretta the widow works in a beauty parlor
she sweeps up hair and perm papers

slinging hash at the diner suits her better
Maureen tries to ignore her mother

Loretta and her girlfriends sit in the kitchen
talking of men their kids going bad and other disasters

Jules sees his mother is frowsy and insubstantial
he wants to protect her but more and more he stays away

Pat moves into the flat his big hands and bad back
between jobs he seldom wears a shirt

Ma Wendell sour and sick watches TV in the dark
Betty pushes her grandmother down the back stairs

sometimes Jules sees Betty running commando in the streets
after school Maureen reads at the library

Loretta confuses her daughters
the good one the bad one cursing them both

drink enhances Loretta's knack for skimming the surface
she's married and pregnant again

her husband stays away from the flat later and later
Maureen's job is to haul him home and fix his supper

at all hours Maureen thinks about money
the household taboo the key to freedom

slender and vague in her school uniform
it's easy to stop a man in a car he opens the door

"Get in, honey" clutching her books she rehearses the act
Smile here Hurry now This is where I go limp

"What's the matter?" "Nothing" "Do you love me?" "Sure"
she stashes the bills in a poetry book where no one will look

but Pat sees Maureen in a car with a man
he finds the money and beats her almost to death

the other Maureen floats as a ghost above the scene
Pat is sentenced to four months in prison

Loretta devotes herself to her invalid daughter
Maureen lies in bed for a year without speaking

eating everything sweet rolls and cookies and cake
finally a letter from Jules wakes Maureen

he doesn't mention Nadine the rich girl from Grosse Point
the one he couldn't leave alone so they ran off together
driving the strangled roads of the Southwest

he doesn't say Nadine left him to die in Texas
he tried to figure things out in the hospital he tells them

but it was a madhouse of interruptions
he put a twenty in the letter "Get Maureen a good doctor"

this doesn't happen instead Maureen wakes on her own
her uncle years on the lam home again brushes her hair

she moves away from her mother and starves herself slender again
enrolls in a course at the University of Detroit

her teacher is Joyce Carol Oates she flunks Maureen
but later responds to her letters "The books you taught us
were mainly lies I can tell you" Maureen writes

Maureen is afraid of everything
men on the street and cars colliding

she needs protection a good husband
she'll fall in love with her English teacher

she'll make him love her he'll leave his wife and kids
as proof he will keep Maureen

Maureen's aim is expert she marries the teacher
they move to a cheap apartment in the suburbs

Jules meanwhile chauffeurs a shadowy client around Detroit
his throat is cut while Jules waits in the car

Jules goes to work for his uncle a rich businessman
they eat lunch in expensive restaurants

in one of these he sees Nadine she's married
they meet in secret at last she gives herself to Jules

they burn up the night
Nadine is black and blue from his love

sunlight glints off luxury cars on the avenue
Nadine shoots Jules twice in the stomach

and then herself but neither one of them dies
the reader's relief is mixed with dread

Jules emerges a gimp half-hearted pimp
courted by leftists

Detroit explodes in the race riots of '67
Loretta's building is looted and burned to the ground

she's thankful for shelter the kindness of strangers
"It makes me feel more alone to think I had kids, and they went off"

she confides to a man his own house burned down
his four children "gone in all directions"

Loretta is shocked to see her son on TV news
dressed in black his voice coarse as a bad wind

"Fire burns and does its duty" Jules shouts at the camera
the son is a murderer the mother turns away weeping

Jules appears at his sister's door in Dearborn
he's come to tell her good-bye he's going to California

"Can I come in?" "No I have a new life"
"Can I meet your husband?" "No he's teaching night school"

Maureen says "You are my brother I love you but please go away"
Jules asks her at least to get in touch with their mother

Maureen refuses she's going to have a baby
her husband has to pay child support there's not enough money

"But men can come back" Jules warns
maybe he means she won't be safe in any case
Jules should know the way he breaks into women

Maureen can see he's the old Jules again
"light on his feet and surprising"

he says he'll get rich in California return to Detroit
and marry Nadine the woman who tried to kill him

Maureen is desperate for him to leave
Jules the only one she loved the railing wobbles under his hand

Maureen repeats she'll never go back to the old life
the reader feels desolate oh the wretched characters

thrashing and grabbing at straws
clenched in the jaws of American history
even their author can't save them

Esquire Haiku

1
Sprawled on piers, sofas,
ice floes, draped & presented
for Gucci, Prada,

Vuitton, Versace:
starved bodies advertising
hip designer drugs

2
"Even the windshield
washer fluid is hot"—Cadillac
Escalade

3
Tiki Barber straddles
a bench, palming a football
like a leather breast

4
One naked blonde &
six pretty boys dressed for the
nineteenth century

one lad on the floor
ruffled shirt, a bullet hole
plugs his golden chest

5
Pg 50: Contents
(Like driving without a map
clear to Iowa)

6
Pg 52: Letters
to the Editor (All things
desired, despised)

7
Beautiful Woman's
joke: So many facelifts her
pubic hair's a goatee

8
Kid leather luggage
tailored suits, ebony skin—
stuff you can envy

9
Review of Cormac
McCarthy's *The Road*: father
son, ash, hunger, death

10
A beautiful girl
on the record: "What I like
in a man is BALLS"

11
Christina Ricci
in *Black Snake Moan,* tight cutoffs
& shitkicker boots

hot look cast over
her shoulder sauntering down
a lone country road

12
The Style Award
goes to fortyish man
sexy in Levi's

13
On eulogies: Don't
read poetry, don't refer
to Bartlett's, don't sing

14
Leggy naked girl
shapes an alpine snow angel
(just drink Evian)

15
Ten Things You Don't Know
About Women: (6) Admire
new bath mat, get laid

16
On men & football:
(10) "Have sex with another dude
once a year instead"

17
A Woman We Love:
Heart-shaped face, black panties, silk
sheets: "Two people need

only three things in
common—sex, food, vacation
destinations"

18
Portrait of Sal &
Mabel Mangano, fiercely
grim, unbeautiful,

charged with negligent
homicide for failure to
evacuate

thirty-five seniors
"drowned like rats" by Katrina
at their nursing home

19
Father with woodcut—
son after Afghanistan
blown up in Iraq

20
Speed-turning pages
now—skip September 11
testimonials

& Ground Zero piece—
after two hundred pages
true life dull as dirt

21
Merv Griffin on red
couch beside Charlie Chaplin
his adored shar-pei—

Eva Gabor would
rise early at his ranch and
stroll down to the barn—

when Merv went down
"every horse in the pasture had
red lipstick on it"

Supper with Jack

A nurse's aide in pink scrubs wheels Jack to our table.
He is wearing black sunglasses,
the aide takes them off.
Jack's eyes are closed—"Jack, wake up!"
Gently she shakes him.
Jack wears a terry-cloth bib from neck to lap
identical to my mother's.
He growls low in his throat—he must have been a lion
in his prime.
"It's suppertime, Jack!"
The aide projects her agenda into his ear,
she rubs and pinches his cheek.
Jack opens his eyes, they are shrunken and dull.
"Open your mouth, Jack!"
She spoons mashed potatoes into the gap:
he closes his eyes against the fact
there's a contract out to keep him alive.
At other tables some of the residents feed themselves;
once they've recovered from surgery
they'll walk out of here
unlike Jack or the brain-damaged man fed by his wife
or two Amazons spoon-fed in oversized wheelchairs

one of them crooning fragments of "Frankie and Johnny."
"Don't fall asleep on me, Jack."
His feeder swipes gravy off his chin; another protest
collects at the back of his throat.
"Arrrgh!" he roars.
My mother frowns, "Do I have to eat all this?"
"Two more bites and a sip of milk," I coax.
She tucks her chin to swallow
the way the physical therapist taught her to do.
Her mouth has grown too small for the spoon;
brussel sprouts roll away from the fork.
"Everything's so much work," my mother complains
"nothing has any taste."
The tissue around her eyes is bruise colored.
"I want to lie down."
"Okay," I say.
"Jack, Jack, open your mouth!" the aide commands.
"Food makes me feel bad," Jack mumbles.
My mother stands
she pushes her walker back from the table
her spine erect as an empress.
She doesn't think to say good-bye to Jack.

Tally

Beyond my sweetheart's blurred profile close on the pillow

four pink tulips in perfect focus.

Six years ago today my country invaded Iraq.

This morning a neighbor laid her husband of sixty years to rest.

The tulips will drop their petals in less than forty-eight hours.

All afternoon the sky has strained to give its rain.

By nightfall the widow will sink into helpless weeping.

New Math

At first you view the catastrophe as a spreadsheet of losses—
but each subtraction or finite collapse elucidates,
through isolation, the fraction remaining.

Charred windmill and crisscrossed fences
frost-studded at dawn. One muezzin crow on a blade
calling the flock—cacophony of response.

Bundle together the twigs at your feet and tie them with yarn.
Launch a flotilla of candlelit boats on a river.
Try again to perceive the shape that wants to be found.

IV

Chicxulub

Into the Wild

(For Christopher McCandless, who went in)

You meet each point in the wild with wild desire—
mountains, caribou, icy current rushing

your waist, a squirrel in your teeth,
the aqua womb of the bus—until, approaching

starvation, a caribou calf appears to you
as a bold parenthesis: inside this, your moose

swarming with maggots, a grizzly's snout,
earth's platter of poisonous greens,

especially the river, lashing you to this teeming,
motherless place.

Charging the Summit

Shrouded in the strobe-light
snows of Everest
one mountaineer sits upright
others toppled
by summit winds
seven climbers lumber past
their kettledrum hearts
funneling air
prisoners banging tin
cups in the lungs
—inhale—exhale—the four
most precious syllables on earth.

Sunlight wands dazzle the air
fifty steps
below
the summit—
a quick calculation: over
or around?
The lead climber steps onto
the silver scales of an escalator
and over the seated
corpse—he doesn't look down
or pause to exhale
the glittering names of the dead.

Javier Makes Landfall

It is a delight to souls to become wet.
—Heraclitus

Javier plucks the grey chords of the sea.
Making landfall in mid-September,
he makes a mess in his exuberance—
trees yanked from gummy ground,
houses and trucks
hurled across town,
river channels
shunted—*tour jetés* and Kung Fu kicks
he frolics across the stage of Baja
and spins north
on a whim—*hasta luego, amigos!*—
scoring the scorpion sands of Jornada del Muerto.

*

Here at the tip of the Southern Rockies
high desert arches her back
to meet him—joy in downpour
weathered by fishermen
rocking in boats
off the coast
of Maine and Nova Scotia.
Matured by default,
nostalgic now for his stint in the womb,
Javier's gestures become expressive—
much as the inmate sentenced to life
turns to yoga or God.

*

Sunday morning Javier drums
a jussive command on our windows and roofs:
Okay, all of you—hotshots, murderers,
lovers, nuns, you with your head
in the noose—go back to bed!
Obediently, we set down our hymnals,
our crayons and measures and cups of brew
and fall entranced onto pallets
and beds, the flesh startled and beautiful.
Straddling the backs of dolphins and whales, we swoon
to sleep in lambent embrace as Javier,
yawning, rains.

Autumn Road to Silver City

Driving west from Magdalena, cliff-face Madonna, hills
threaded with zinc and lead, the moss greens of cedar and oak
melt into prairie grasses. Twenty-seven radio towers,
steel giants stationed on tracks, swivel to catch the strains
of celestial music. Antelope lope behind a fence; zigzag
trail of ranch trucks; a lone windmill.

The Plains of San Agustín receive the road like flaxen palms
opening out to God. My sweetheart is telling me what he knows
about breeds of cattle: whiteface Herefords,
a lazy lot, low on maternal instinct; Texas longhorns,
hearty but unpredictable; the jutted shoulders of dairy cows,
trusses for pendulous udders.

Hills spill from golden tops and roll to stillness, shored by crimson
grasses. Old Horse Springs and the road
descends, wends through stands of yellow aspen,
opens at Apache Creek where bands of defiant Chiricahuas
eluded U.S. Cavalry troops and wintered in peace,
starving and freezing.

Timbered slopes give way to the town of Reserve. TGIF!
Miners, loggers and two-stepping cowgirls
beat the setting sun to the punch—trucks lined like rows of shoes
outside of Ella's Café and a tavern across the road.
We stop the car at the locked gate of a cemetery. Empty barges
behind bars, a double tombstone's plastic carnations

shape the twin endearments, "Mom" and "Dad."
Here beside the Frisco River, Elfego Baca, law-and-order man
from Socorro, held off a mob of cattle rustlers for thirty-three hours,
killed three Texans. The road leads to a rickety bridge, creeks

and meadows carved on a sign; we turn around and drive
too far in the other direction.

Hometown girls walk the hill, their backs to Reserve.
Smiling for nothing, they turn us around.
Tire and axle read by Braille the darkened lay of the land.
Saliz Pass and the tiny downhill village of Alma; past the turnoff
for Mogollon, screaming head-on ambulance lights
scrape vertiginous curves.

Inside the Glenwood Chevron station
an elderly woman, brittle and trembling,
asks which town have I come from.
"Alma."
"You passed the ambulance then?"
"Yes."
"Was there an accident?"
"Not that we saw."
Her small hands console each other.
"*Ojalá!*" (invoking Allah), "I pray nobody is hurt."

Approaching Silver City from the west, city lights cluster together
like stars the Trickster has tossed into the sky.
Billy the Kid was a boy in these streets, cut wide for cattle drives,
curbed high against floods. The B & B sits on a knoll,
octogenarian shaded by giant maples.
Wooden steps groan as we climb. Behind us abide

the colors of grasses, secrets of villages, girls on a road
smiling at dusk, *abuela* doing gas station vigil,
worried that someone has died.

Autobiography of an Itinerant

Strange to tell I knew from the start
I wouldn't cross the bridge—

I'd pedal the backbone of mountains,
the tender arc of jungles,

circling the globe at a diligent pace,
each step a renewed commitment

to fate, destination
the problem of balance and falling.

Dream On: Beds from Asia to Europe

The night guard at the Museum of International Folk Art
knows who we are: off-duty locals lulled to our senses by beds
of the world—low sleepers in Borneo, high sleepers in Indonesia,
Greek, Uzbek, Norwegian cocoons for sleeping on the move.

He watches us glide like somnolent ducks from lily to lily.
Inside these rooms we are experts on sleep, aficionados
of tasseled kilim, goat hair valise, silken duvet,
pillows of bamboo and jade. He understands

how we want to caress—burnished grasses and gossamer
threads; orchid tendrils stitched into quilted fields;
we would scorch our hands on Turkish weaves
like autumn leaves burning.

He trawls us, our guard, in the dark net of his eyes. Our faces
migrate steamily close to henna and indigo dyes, the clean
cottons of Finland. Our sentry knows we would fling ourselves
down on bridal futon, Parisian four-poster, cushions strewn

in a pasha's tent for odalisque harem. His shimmering bride
steps from her bath as he guards against our subliminal urge
to climb into hand-painted cradle (Swiss, circa 1800)
and dream in its maple embrace.

Travel Moods

(i)

Gather up disturbances: The low ritual of airport security,
slabs of ham in a B & B basement, your dank room
at the top. You buy a thing you already know
you're not going to want. Crush of
sweat and cheap cologne on rush-hour trains—
the world has gone to cellular chat and youthful insouciance.
One map has a critical gap, another a double identity.
Caught in a city's hostile wind, your blood sugar
plummets, you blame your traveling companion.
How have you squandered the years of your life
that you don't speak a word of the language?
Nerves ache like rotting teeth, the tongue refuses to move.
Backtrack across the chilled Atlantic in sullen silence. . . .
All this you ball up and shove into darkness,
back of your hall closet.

(ii)

The Queen is in, the Royal Standard flies over Buckingham
Palace. Children loosed on Trafalgar Square
sprawl in the marble laps of statesmen.
A hawk released by Bird Control
swoops to Admiral Nelson's hat and snaps
the necks of polluting pigeons.
Kidney pie and draft beer in dark leather pub.
David Hockney's towering blue humans.
A schoolboy at the British Museum
poses beside a mummy for his mommy. (Blink
and his baby fat fast-forwards to bone.)
The Polynesian God A'a (provocative for Freud and Picasso)
hums from a hollowed belly.
The crowd around the Rosetta Stone

would touch, if they could, the delicate tonnage.
A matinee at the National Theatre
floods you with pathos, a second with dark joy.
Carpe diem! Cross the muscular back of the Thames
buoyed by lights and fellow travelers babbling in tongues.

(iii)
Your Swiss friend points up at the oldest house in Luzern.
Seven hundred years later a blonde leans from a top window,
pruning geraniums tumbled against the wood.

(iv)
Summit Italian Alps in fog, crawling on four wheels.
Seventeenth-century granite village
haloed by frozen falls. Summer families
returned to the city, one old woman carries
a bucket, one old man a shovel.
Painted tableaus along the road, Mary and Jesus
in faded stone dresses.

(v)
Green hills lifted above the curves of Lake Maggiore,
a brown puppy trots to the end of the pier.
Glass voices of two rowers break against the air.
Champagne and figs on the balcony; the maid cleaning
the room next door is singing.

(vi)
Standing in line for Customs Inspection,
an African woman smiles at you across fluorescent chasms—
you, impartially blessed by beauty!

Traveling Companions
(For Elizabeth and Leo)

Not like a centipede straggling along
in one organized body,
angling for food,
a place to lay the legs—
but more like waves breaking,
the one broken
receding into
the one incoming.
Leo and Elizabeth eating breakfast
at a diner in Bullfrog, Utah:
"I wish the sea was not so far away."
"Yes, too bad."
Back in the car the one at the wheel
turns due west.

Great Sand Dunes

(i)

Packing to leave I'm already thinking of coming back to Max
the feeble cat and hollyhock seedlings shriveling in the heat
not to mention my credit card dropped in a parking lot
when we were giddy together making light of gravity's clout
the replacement hasn't arrived and thus my key to gas pumps
and roadside diners is flying over Kansas back home to a new
book its pages glistening like snowfields cut flowers clean sheets
such dissolves from the mind wheeling on petroleum wings
through sage and flaxen grasslands dark-edged with cedar
blue benevolent sky and clouds like down pillows especially
once we reach the dunes heaving exactly like waves of the sea
"but for the color" wrote Zebulon Pike in 1907 charting the dunes
known by feel to Utes and Apaches the dune just under our feet
hiding from view the others

(ii)

A woman brushing her teeth in front of metallic restroom mirror
tells me a bear strolled across the back of their campground
a black bear not a grizzly we didn't see a bear along the river trail
a western tanager dove at our heads in an aspen clearing
protecting his eggs or chicks and after sunup near the stream
that rims the sands deer grazing in groups of six or seven
we climb the dunes barefooted towards the top on all fours
at six hundred feet the highest dunes in North America nothing
grows or visibly moves on the surface but little rivers of sand
cascade wherever we step like whispering insects it's good says Tom
that humans cannot undo the dunes the wind erases our steps
afternoon clouds brushing the mounds in lush mauve shadow
we sit facing the sand mountains on plastic folding chairs
darkness swirls its magician's coat the greatest show on earth

(iii)

Three boys are playing stickball in the campground the youngest
shows me a caterpillar the ones with spiky fur will turn into moths
not butterflies he insists the "s's" hiss through gaps in his teeth
my sister encamped all month at the dunes is washing forks
we pack our gear she'll be "nesting and resting" the rest of the day
she and I compare the state of our knees mine wrenched years ago
hiking down a mountain hers needing ice now inhabiting the body
a game of diminishing returns "the thousand natural shocks
that flesh is heir to" near Manassa the birthplace of Jack Dempsey
a plume of smoke fanned by winds below the San Juan range
a trio of silvery rivers near Española and Santa Fe's soft breath
inside the house the cat is bawling his old voice worn to a rasp
accidentally closed in a room he must have cried for three days
while we were at large cavorting

Ten Dancers Containing the Universe
(For the Aspen Santa Fe Ballet dancers)

Each dancer's solar plexus cups a bowl of stars
            a bound seed
                        guzzling space
                                    avalanche gathering speed
            hot stars centrifugally
whirling the cosmos

Legs split like arrows leaving the bow
            bodies lifting and falling
                        as spores
                                    or meteors
                        we loosen our breath
            their bullet feet
spinning the planet

Full Circle

The Full Circle Ceremony was an international action initiated by Japanese Buddhist monks to extinguish the burning embers of Hiroshima and Nagasaki at Trinity Site, New Mexico, on August 9, 2005.

(i)

As for the smoldering caldron we call the world,
Japanese monks hold it in their hands.

Abbot Ota carried a box from Nagasaki
consecrated to cradle atomic ashes

and Buddhist monks in black robes
walked from San Francisco to Trinity Site:

they ferried a flame in a red lantern
kindled from Hiroshima's burning embers.

(ii)

Late in the day a cloudburst shines the air.
Twelve monks face the monolith, sixty years

stationed at Ground Zero; they kneel
on little satin boats afloat on the desert floor

and offer silent prayers. To the west, a luminous
storm swirls above the San Mateos

and on our faces a breeze so clement,
we who are watching barely need to breathe.

(iii)
Abbot Ota holds a chain of paper cranes
folded with the prayers of southwestern children:

Please, please, never again a nuclear bomb
dropped on creatures anywhere in the world!

He bundles the cranes in the prayer cloth.
Three monks wrap it with string;

tenderly, they feed it to the atomic flame
set on the ground to burn.

(iv)
Under extravagant summer sky nothing moves
but breath, blaze, the sandy lights of grama grass

and white blossoming yucca. The ravenous flame
consumes itself to ashes.

The Rooster Pull

(i)
Inside the church painted with turquoise horses
Pueblo women serve a revolving feast
and all afternoon men on horseback race for roosters
dangled from poles in the plaza.
Shaded by cottonwoods, mothers and grandmothers
sit along the acequia watching with soft attention—
children playing, barefoot boys wrestling for roosters,
blur of jousting horsemen. Late in the day, rain
spatters the dust; sun makes its hot finale.
The roosters are finished. The horsemen bring
toys to the children and circle the church, tossing
cornmeal into the yard. We pack up our chairs
and retrace the lazy two-lane road to the interstate.

(ii)
The cloud symphony's brass section rises
to its feet over the mountains.
A lone farmhouse slumps beside the highway.
Back of the mind a chorus of strangled voices
argues for the sanctity of all
sentient beings. Each culture invents its rules
and none resolve the contradictions—look
at us now, speeding through
beauty . . . wide blue gaze of sky
spilling into a silver gap along the horizon.
Three vultures scoop a caldron of air.
How red the roosters' fertile blood and deep
the shadows, delivered on platters of light!

Chicxulub

Six miles across and careening nine to twelve miles per second
the asteroid Chicxulub tore through earth's atmosphere
gouging the sea somewhere off the Yucatán Peninsula
searing on impact Cretaceous fishes, green-eating Iguanodon,
Tyrannosaurus gnashing samurai teeth. Cheek-shoo-loob
(so named by mortals) pulverized the planet's sands, fewer
in number than galaxies burning the heavens.

* * *

Leaping away from flame and smoke
    screams entombed in concrete and steel
        we fall in a basket of velvet air
    wind balloons the body
stalling the sure descent
    somebody's hand holding mine
        equal pressure of inner and outer
            never on earth was there so much time
    we're wafting down towards tiny
humans fleeing the towers
    buckled and roaring with smoke
        the terror of what they have lost
            the things they must still destroy
        they can't imagine the sweetness of falling
    sidewalk squares stippled with saplings
magnolia leaves mapping the planet
        my falling partner
    squeezes my hand
and releases.

* * *

The Costa Rican tour guide hands a miniature flashlight
to each of the girls: "Aim your light at the ground."
Every inch of tropical earth glistens with tiny lights.
"Spider eyes," he says.

* * *

150 million years after the Permian Sea sifted to desert sand,
American Indians paved this trail with turquoise,
feathers, arrowheads, blue and yellow corn. In 1540
conquistadors seeking cities of gold glittered the path
with horseshoes and nails, pieces of broken armor.
Franciscan friars stirred the dust with breviaries and bells.
Merchants followed with buckets, harnesses, coffins,
ticking for shawls, bolts of cloth for the brides.

* * *

Mexican gardener raking gravel
smooth to the edges of granite fountains
flashes his radiant smile.

Yoga students lie on the floor in corpse pose,
watching the spaces between the strokes of the rake
empty and fill with their breath.

The gardener watches pebbles
settle, nesting doves in fountain grass, a sky
summoning rain.

* * *

Eight hundred feet below the bridge
the Rio Grande in its lava sleeve

a bald eagle fishes the river
an easy leap from raptor soaring to earth
convulsion—pelvis and hips
hard-jam the black isosceles portholes
a startled body could fall through.

* * *

Pyotr Ilyich Tchaikovsky was gnawed in his heart by a worm. Some say he wept like a child, fearing he'd die as his mother had of cholera. Early on he conducted an orchestra holding his chin in his left hand to keep his head from tumbling off his shoulders. The composer died in St. Petersburg, in 1893, of cholera.

* * *

One of the bones in the child's wrist snapped clean
has a name you remember—"ulna"—
flat and white as a Peloponnesian road,
but what is the word for the sentry bone
below the little finger? Memory
like sandbags propping the banks of a river,
ropes of willow teasing over the torrent . . .
If only you could grab hold of a clay animal
bulging out of the bank and stroke its slippery
haunch—might the earth take you back?

* * *

A small visitor to the pueblo sits on his mother's lap.
Dancers and drummers wheel on top of the earth
like a giant insect. Under yellow sun and NY Giants cap
the child is eating a snow cone. Toadstool umbrellas,

purple and green and red, float overhead. "The drums
make my heart feel good," he says.

* * *

A man from Elwood, Indiana, walked away from a lottery game with $57,000. "I'm very thankful," he beamed into the camera, "now I can buy a very nice car." Hours later, crossing the street to the neighborhood store where he'd purchased the winning ticket, Carl D. Atwood, 73, was struck by a pickup truck. Rushed to the nearest hospital, he died in the afternoon.

* * *

Clouds shattered by sunlight: Aphrodite
rising out of her half shell.

* * *

Bulbs of light puncture the dusk over Hartford.
Someone down there is dying.
A householder lays a fire, strikes a match
with his thumbnail.
An adolescent reading a textbook
superimposes women's bodies over the pages.
A woman speaks in soft, apologetic tones
to the dead in the cemetery.
Alone in the woods, a baritone bellows "Ave Maria"
to snow-laden trees.

* * *

No love can be discounted.

* * *

Every other week, one of the planet's 7,000
extant languages
dies out.

Language a nest egg
                                        a minefield
                                                        a cave studded with rubies.

Choose a handful of nouns at random:
            oxbow
                        egg
                                    newspaper
                        lizard
            collision

Relinquish the concept of random.

* * *

A prankster hangs a noose from the ceiling while his roommate sleeps.
Play it again. This time he won't take the bait.
The young man gets out of bed and works to loosen the hard knot
            in the dark.

* * *

Dry heat muffles your feet,
the parched plains of your face.

All night motionless falling
swallows the fifth dimension.

Your tongue scraped of acid and honey
angles for water.

Dawn at last comes to the well—
her stone basin, her bolt of dark hair.

* * *

Faulknerian wrinkles in family history won't iron out.
But don't you find there is freedom in knowing that fate
doubles back, tosses you into its bone cart and rumbles on?
We step without knowing the ground beneath our feet.
And yet I am here, the tracks behind me are mine.

* * *

Hawara checkpoint, south of Jerusalem, March 25, 2004:
Israeli checkpoint soldiers, perceiving a lump
under a Palestinian's jacket, order the youth to freeze.
A robot extends a pair of scissors to cut free his vest.
The high school boy is wired to blow. Although he has
longed for a river of honey, a river of wine and seventy-two
virgins, young Hussam Abdo declined to flip the switch.
"When the soldiers stopped me," he tells a reporter,
"I changed my mind, I didn't want to die anymore,
I'm sorry for what I did."

* * *

Imagine that you are being observed benevolently.

* * *

Growing fat, the moon's talons
claw and drag.
                                        Eclipsing,
she strokes our waning bodies
with pearl fingers.

* * *

You probably didn't mean what you said, you were
tired or drunk. But don't forget that points are deducted
for sending an innocent flying backwards into the void.

* * *

In four-wheel drive we follow the archaeologist out
to the site of a silicified rhyolite quarry
west of Socorro.
Paleolithic peoples traveled here from all directions
to fashion weapons and tools.
Bent like storks, our boots
crunching umber shale, we're searching for ridges,
concussions, scrapers, cleavers,
an arrowhead maybe.
The sun moves faster than we do up the hill.
At the top, a single volcanic rock outcropping,
cathedral for sleeping snakes. Mesas encircling the valley
are stubbled with sage and supple April light.

* * *

Firemen bang on the woman's door
below the ridge where the fire rages.
The wind has changed directions—
she must evacuate right away—

they can save her house or her barn,
but not both. The woman chooses
to save the house and shuts
her horses in the kitchen
with food and water.

* * *

Nature is ever optimistic, Jay Harman insists. A green
inventor himself, he shares Gaia's enthusiasm for
seashells, hurricanes, golden spirals, the graceful cycles
of lava, seaweed, glacier, bloodstream, gulf stream.
Where we are obsessed with ice caps melting and spewed
petroleum gagging dolphins and fishes, the optimist
ponders blades of grass breaking through asphalt
seeds and spores sprung to life, a new strain of microbe—
designer bugs gobbling toxins, microorganisms deftly
outsmarting genetic modifications. There's far more profit
in copying nature than in its destruction. Look around, he
says. Our earth can show us how to heal our wounds.

Notes

"Ashes"

A series of wildfires swept across Southern California in October 2007 and burned half a million acres from Santa Barbara County to the U.S.-Mexico border. The fire destroyed some 1,500 homes and at least 500,000 people were evacuated. The particular fire referred to in "Ashes" was the Harris fire in southeastern San Diego County. (This is the same fire that burned around the horses in the kitchen in "Chicxulub.")

"Love in the Afternoon"

Thanks to Sue Mingus for granting permission to use the song title, "Love is a Dangerous Necessity" as an epigraph (from Charles Mingus's recording *Charles Mingus in Paris*, Sunnyside Records, recorded October 31, 1970, in Paris).

"The Summer Pages"

To force a decisive end to World War II, the United States dropped atomic bombs on Hiroshima and Nagasaki, Japan, on August 6 and August 9, 1945. These devices were dubbed "Little Boy" and "Fat Man" by their creators.

"Javier Makes Landfall"

Hurricane Javier was the strongest storm of the 2004 Pacific hurricane season with winds blowing at 150 miles an hour. Because of wind shear in the East Pacific, Javier weakened to the level of a tropical storm before making landfall in Baja California in late September. Javier dumped 3.3 inches of rain in Arizona and 1–3 inches over New Mexico, Colorado, Texas, and Utah, mitigating severe drought conditions in the Southwest. Since Javier caused minimal damage on land, the World Meteorological Organization did not retire the name Javier but retained it on the list to be used for the 2010 Pacific hurricane season.

"Charging the Summit"
Mount Everest has been called the highest mountain and the biggest graveyard in the world. Close to two hundred climbers have died on Everest and most of those remain where they fell. Frozen bodies that have not been buried under avalanches are sometimes visible to climbers nearing the summit, but high altitude, low oxygen, intense cold, and winds make it nearly impossible for the living to haul the dead bodies back down the mountain.

"The Rooster Pull"
The rooster pull, or gallo, is a ritual game on horseback practiced in midsummer by several Indian pueblos along the Rio Grande. It is thought to be an ancient fertility rite introduced to Southwestern pueblos by Spanish conquistadors in the 1600s. Over the centuries, the gallo became woven into Pueblo Indian religious rites and beliefs and is usually preceded by a Catholic mass and religious procession. The rooster pull varies in format from village to village. Sometimes a rooster is dangled from a crossbar; sometimes it's buried up to its neck in the ground; either way, galloping horsemen make a grab for it. The rooster gets pulled apart, the winner accrues a spiritual blessing, and the earth is fertilized by rooster blood. In recent years, animal rights activists have tried to put a stop to the sacrificial rite. In response, the pueblos sometimes choose to close the event to the public.

"Full Circle"
On August 9, 2005, Japanese Buddhist monks extinguished embers from the atomic bombing of Hiroshima in a ceremony near Alamogordo, New Mexico. For sixty years, monks had carried a red lantern containing a flame kindled by the atomic bomb in peace marches around the world. The lantern contained three flames, representing Trinity Site, Hiroshima, and Nagasaki. In Buddhist thought, sixty years completes a cycle. At Trinity Site, beneath the obelisk marking the birth of the atomic bomb, a dozen monks sat on the desert floor and passed the lantern around their circle. Then they lit a torch from each of the three flames and Abbot Ota extinguished the flame in the lantern. The monks touched their torches to a rolled prayer

cloth covered with origami peace cranes made by children in Arizona and New Mexico. As the flame burned out, they prayed that nuclear weapons would never again be used against humanity. The ceremony ended at twilight. Ashes and dirt were scooped up and put in a box with four compartments: three were for Hiroshima, Nagasaki, and a museum in the United States, and the fourth would be divided and sent to the heads of countries with nuclear capability, including the United States.

"Chicxulub"
Chicxulub is the name of a crater geophysicists believe was made by a meteor that struck the Yucatán Peninsula about sixty-five million years ago at the end of the Cretaceous period. The Mayan name roughly translates as "the tail of the devil." The exploding fireball was at least six miles in diameter and carved a crater more than 110 miles across. The meteor's impact may have caused the extinction of the dinosaurs and would have set off some of the largest mega-tsunamis in Earth's history—waves thousands of feet high. Scientists call impacts of Chicxulub's magnitude "civilization enders."

Acknowledgments

Some of these poems appeared in the following publications, print and electronic:

"Catch and Release," "How Shadows Are Bundled," "Notes to a Man Who Is Thinking of Leaving His Wife," "Up in the Dark," and "Writing a Poem" in *POEM: Poets on Exchange Mission*

"Ashes," "Supper with Jack," and "Charging the Summit" in *Lunarosity*

"Things That Want to Be Counted" in *Santa Fe Literary Review*

"Dream On: Beds from Asia to Europe" and "Loving Dick Cheney" in *Sin Fronteras/Writers without Borders*

"Full Circle" in *Southwestcrossroads: Cultures and Histories of the American Southwest.org*

"Autumn Road to Silver City" in *El Palacio: Art, History, and Culture of the Southwest*